Tell Me Why

WHY?

I Get Hungry

Katie Marsico

Published in the United States of America by Cherry Lake Publishing
Ann Arbor, Michigan
www.cherrylakepublishing.com

Content Adviser: Lisa K. Militello, PhD, MPH, CPNP, The Ohio State University
Reading Adviser: Marla Conn, ReadAbility, Inc.

Photo Credits: © bonzodog/Shutterstock Images, cover, 1, 13; © Samuel Borges Photography/
Shutterstock Images, cover, 1, 15; © rmnoa357/Shutterstock Images, cover, 1, 19; © Monkey Business
Images/Shutterstock Images, cover, 1, 5, 13, 17, 19; © NADKI/Shutterstock Images, cover, 1, 21;
© vita khorzhevska/Shutterstock Images, 7; © 3drenderings/Shutterstock Images, 9; © Gladskikh Tatiana/
Shutterstock Images, 11; © Olga Rosi/Shutterstock Images, 15;

Library of Congress Cataloging-in-Publication Data

Marsico, Katie, 1980-
 I get hungry / by Katie Marsico.
    pages cm. -- (Tell me why)
"Young children are naturally curious about themselves. Tell Me Why I Get Hungry offers answers to
their most compelling questions about their rumbling tummy. Age-appropriate explanations and
appealing photos encourage readers to continue their quest for knowledge. Additional text features and
search tools, including a glossary and an index, help students locate information and learn new words."
—Provided by publisher.
 Audience: Ages 6-10.
 Audience: Grades K to Grade 3.
 Includes bibliographical references and index.
 ISBN 978-1-63188-994-3 (hardcover) -- ISBN 978-1-63362-072-8 (pdf) -- ISBN
978-1-63362-033-9 (pbk.) -- ISBN 978-1-63362-111-4 (ebook) 1.
Children--Nutrition--Juvenile literature. I. Title.

RJ206.M2792 2015
613.2083--dc23
                                          2014031779

Cherry Lake Publishing would like to acknowledge the work of The Partnership for 21st Century Skills.
Please visit *www. p21.org* for more information.

Printed in the United States of America
Corporate Graphics

Table of Contents

Is Dinner Done Yet?................................4

Sending Signals...................................10

A Silent Stomach.................................14

Handling Hunger Pangs......................18

Think About It....................................22

Glossary...23

Find Out More....................................23

Index...24

About the Author...............................24

Is Dinner Done Yet?

When's dinner going to be ready? That's what Andre keeps wondering. He is trying to do his homework at the kitchen table. But it's hard to focus on math. His stomach is achy and growling.

Andre ate a big lunch at school. So why is he getting hungry now? Andre decides to ask his dad—right after he finds out how much longer their pasta needs to cook!

We often feel hungry when we haven't eaten in a while.

Andre's dad says that hunger is the body's **reaction** to its need for food. He explains that this is different from appetite. Appetite makes people want to eat certain foods that look, smell, or taste good. Hunger is about the body *needing* food for **nutrients**. Living things rely on nutrients to grow and stay healthy.

We eat dessert to satisfy our appetite for sweets.

A person's **digestive system** breaks down food into nutrients and waste. It is made up of **organs** such as the stomach and **intestines**. When people are hungry, they sometimes experience hunger pangs in these parts of their body.

A hunger pang is a feeling of mild discomfort. Tiredness, dizziness, and mood changes are other signs of hunger. So are groaning or grumbling noises that sound like they're coming from your stomach.

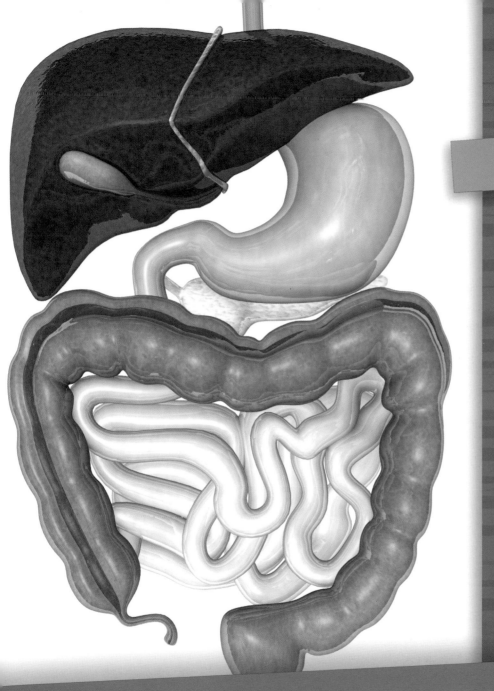

Look at this picture of the human digestive system. Do you see the stomach and intestines?

You may have felt hunger pangs in your digestive system.

Sending Signals

Beep! The oven timer signals that dinner is ready. Andre jokes that his stomach is definitely sending him a signal, too! But Dad says that hunger involves far more than his digestive system.

Hunger has its beginnings in the brain. Messages are sent to the brain from the body. These messages reveal how the body will use the food. They also contain information about how full the stomach and intestines are.

Your brain and stomach let you know when it's time to eat.

The brain uses these details to create signals that travel back to the digestive system. In turn, muscles in the stomach and intestines begin to contract, or squeeze. When the stomach and intestines are full, this squeezing keeps food moving throughout the body. When they're empty, however, such contractions create hunger pangs.

ASK QUESTIONS!

How do your brain and digestive system work together to let you know when you're full? Ask your family doctor!

A healthy snack can help keep you from getting too hungry between meals.

A Silent Stomach

Ah, what a delicious dinner! Once he starts eating, Andre notices that his stomach stops rumbling. Why did it growl in the first place?

Dad surprises Andre by saying that a grumbling stomach isn't always a sign of hunger. Contractions don't just push food through the digestive system. They also squeeze gases such as air back and forth. This movement causes what are sometimes noisy **vibrations**.

Burping is another noise that involves the digestive system. Are you able to guess why people burp?

Burping is a noise we sometimes make after eating.

Stomach grumbles tend to be quieter when food is being digested. Andre's dad compares it to shouting in a crowded room versus an empty room. It's easier to hear the shout in an empty room because there are no other sounds. That's why growling sounds seem louder when people are hungry. Their stomach and intestines are empty!

Eating healthy food is the best way to quiet a growling stomach.

Handling Hunger Pangs

As they finish eating, Dad reminds Andre that hunger is usually a normal part of digestion. Still, there's no reason to come to the dinner table starving. Experts recommend that kids eat every 3 to 4 hours during the day.

This equals roughly three meals and two snacks. This supports a healthy **metabolism**.

Having meals on a regular schedule can help you fight hunger pangs.

Eating fruits, vegetables, **lean** meats, beans, and **whole grains** is another way to deal with hunger pangs. These foods are more filling than foods high in sugar and fat. Drinking water throughout the day often eases hunger pangs, too.

By the end of dinner, Andre has a better understanding of why he gets hungry. Thanks to Dad's cooking, Andre also has a full stomach!

Healthy foods are filling and help keep us from getting hungry too fast.

Think About It

People have been known to survive for around 3 weeks without food. Think about the longest you've gone without food. How hungry did you feel?

Have you ever heard the saying, "My eyes were bigger than my stomach"? It describes what happens when people take more food than they're able to eat. Think about how this expression shows the difference between hunger and appetite!

Glossary

digestive system (dye-JESS-tiv SIS-tuhm) the body system responsible for breaking down food into nutrients and waste

intestines (in-TESS-tuhnz) tube-shaped organs that help digest food after it leaves the stomach

lean (LEEN) containing little fat

metabolism (muh-TAB-uh-liz-uhm) the process in our bodies that changes the food we eat into the energy we need to breathe, digest, and grow

nutrients (NU-tree-uhnts) substances that living things need to grow and stay healthy

organs (OR-guhnz) body parts such as the stomach and intestines that perform a specific job

reaction (ree-AK-shuhn) a response

vibrations (vye-BRAY-shuhnz) groups of small, fast movements that follow a back-and forth or side-to-side pattern

whole grains (HOLE GRAYNZ) grains that have not been stripped of any parts or nutrients

Find Out More

Books:

Etingoff, Kim. *Healthy Alternatives to Sweets and Snacks.* Philadelphia: Mason Crest, 2014.

Halvorson, Karin. *Inside the Stomach.* Minneapolis: ABDO Publishing Company, 2013.

Hartman, Eve, and Wendy Meshbesher. *Digestion and Nutrition: What Happens to the Food We Eat?* Chicago: Capstone Raintree, 2014.

Web Sites:

KidsHealth—Your Digestive System
http://kidshealth.org/kid/htbw/digestive_system.html
Find out more about how food gets digested once you eat it!

WebMD FIT—"What's Your Mind Got to Do with Eating?"
http://fit.webmd.com/kids/food/article/mindful-eating
Read an article about the effect your brain has on how you experience hunger.

Index

appetite, 6-7, 22

brain, 10-13
burp, 15

contractions, 12, 14

digestion, 18
digestive system, 8-10, 12-15

eating, 4-5, 18-21

full, 12-13, 20

healthy, 13, 17, 20-21
hunger pangs, 8, 12, 18-20

intestines, 8-10, 12

metabolism, 18
muscles, 12

nutrients, 6, 8

organs, 8-9

reaction, 6

stomach, 4, 8-12, 20
stomach grumbles, 4, 14, 16-17

vibrations, 14

About the Author

Katie Marsico is the author of more than 150 children's books. She lives in a suburb of Chicago, Illinois, with her husband and children.